The Goody-Goody Trap

Scared to Disagree, Guilty to Say No, Panic in Awkward Moments,

Unable to Counter Indirect Talk.

AF660568

"A powerful reflection on the silent emotional slavery we live every day — and a gentle guide to reclaiming your voice, your space, and ability to own your life."

Sanjay Godara

BlueRose ONE.com
Stories Matter
NewDelhi • London

BLUEROSE PUBLISHERS
India | U.K.

BlueRose ONE.com
Stories Matter
New Delhi • London

For permissions requests or inquiries regarding this publication, please contact:

BLUEROSE PUBLISHERS
www.BlueRoseONE.com
info@bluerosepublishers.com
+91 8882 898 898
+4407342408967

ISBN: 978-93-7310-736-3

Cover design: Yash Singhal
Typesetting: Namrata Saini

First Edition: September 2025

Dedication

- To my beloved wife and best friend, **Ritu**,

  who taught me the profound value of intent, kindness, and compassion. Your unwavering love and support have been my sanctuary throughout this journey.

- To my grandmother**, Bhanwari Devi**,

  whose early teachings during my school days planted seeds of wisdom and strength that blossom in every page.

- To my brother-like friend, **Ankit Khandelwal**,

  with whom I shared countless heartfelt conversations and who exemplifies honesty in accepting emotions.

- To my dear college friend, **Apurwa Sarwajit**,

  whose friendship inspired me and from whom I learned so much.

This book stands as a tribute to each of you, whose presence and guidance have shaped both the pages and the person behind them.

Who is this Book For?

This book focuses on something most people never talk about — the invisible "goody-goody trap". It is a pattern where people try to keep everything smooth on the surface, but inside, they are silently suffering.

To keep others comfortable or to avoid tension, they often:

1. Get scared to disagree, even when they truly don't agree.
2. Feel a strange mix of fear and guilt when saying 'No', even when it's the right thing to do.
3. Become anxious and uneasy during awkward moments, and try to escape as quickly as possible.
4. Feel helpless and trapped in indirect conversations, often ending up as the victim without even knowing what happened.

If you are someone who doesn't get disturbed by these things...

Or if you are able to easily navigate such situations — ***Then this book is not meant for you.***

You are already doing fine. You are blessed with this ability to manage discomfort and protect your space. I'm truly happy for you.

But there are some of us — people like me — for whom these moments are not small

This suffering is not just momentary. It's deep and painful.

It affects our self-esteem. It changes how we look at ourselves.

We feel weak, helpless, or ashamed — even when we've done nothing wrong.

This book is for those people.

For the ones who walk away from a conversation with a heavy heart.

For the ones who overthink for hours because they couldn't speak up.

For the ones who want to live with honesty and presence, but keep collapsing under guilt, fear, or awkwardness.

In this book, we will go through three phases:

1. Realization—Understanding what's really happening and why we feel trapped.
2. Recognition—Identifying the specific patterns that cause emotional pain.
3. Becoming—Building the ability to face these emotions and respond with strength.

We'll take this journey slowly and gently — step by step — not by forcing change, but by understanding ourselves better and growing from within.

If you feel this kind of emotional pain and want to stop carrying it silently...

Then yes — this book is for you.

Preface

We often focus on things far away — some big goal, some higher purpose, some distant vision of a meaningful life. But in doing so, we miss the most obvious things right in front of us — the things that are actually affecting us every single day.

We keep ourselves busy watching motivational videos, spiritual talks, or listening to philosophers. But at the same time, we are completely failing to handle the small moments where we feel weak or stuck — like when we can't say "no" to someone, when we're too scared to disagree, when an awkward silence makes us anxious, or when someone talks indirectly and we don't know how to respond. We feel like victims — again and again — and still avoid facing what's really happening.

I'm not here to talk about what is the purpose of life or what is the ultimate goal. These questions are endless, and honestly, they can trap you. Thinking about them makes you feel like you're doing something important, like you're just a few steps away from discovering some great truth. It gives the illusion that you're on the verge of something big — that you're about to win the world. But in reality, you're just running in circles while ignoring the discomfort that's already eating you from within.

These may look like small things from the outside, but the truth is — they shape how we feel about ourselves. And when we can't handle them, we keep losing confidence silently.

When I experienced these things, I couldn't ignore them. They hit me deeply. I kept asking myself — Why do I do something I clearly don't want to do? Why can't I speak up? And at one point, it felt like a kind of emotional slavery — where someone else controls your choices, and you just follow along because you're scared to upset anyone.

This book is not about finding the "meaning of life." It's about facing the small but powerful struggles that we keep ignoring — the things that quietly steal our space, our voice, and our peace of mind.

I wrote this because I needed to understand these things for myself. And if you've also felt trapped in such moments — not because you're weak, but because no one ever taught you how to deal with them — then maybe this book will help you feel a little lighter, a little stronger.

We don't need to fix everything in life. But we must stop ignoring what's hurting us daily — right here, right now.

— Sanjay Godara

Contents

Simply Focusing on What Is Directly Impacting Us

We all at some point start to explore the deeper meaning of our lives and often find ourselves turning to motivational speakers, spiritual gurus, and philosophers.

Someone talks about how to become successful and wealthy. The next moment, someone else says, "Don't chase material success." Then a philosopher comes and talks about finding the 'meaning of life'. Someone else mentions enlightenment and says achieving that stage is the only true path.

With all these different perspectives, we try to choose a path for ourselves. We keep analysing: Which path is right for me? What is the highest goal?

In the process of chasing these grand ideas, we often forget the present-day factors that are directly impacting our daily lives and making us feel like we do not own our space, our voice, and our ground.

People are dominating our lives, and we simply cannot counter that. When we face these uncomfortable situations and feel like victim, we brush them off, **thinking that choosing a grand life path is somehow more important**.

Some people may even argue that these things are small and can be ignored. But I strongly disagree. It may be small for the people who are on the winning side — but not for the ones who suffer from it, like I faced it a lot.

If you cannot feel the owner of your life and end up feeling like a victim of another person's actions, it greatly impacts the way you look at yourself and reduces your self-esteem.

It's not that these higher ideas of life — like 'meaning of life' or 'purpose of life' — are wrong. **But they are secondary.**

First, we need to deal with the parts of life that are in front of us right now — the situations that make us lose our voice, lose our space, and feel helpless.

Once we become strong in these areas — once we are able to speak clearly, hold our ground, and stay calm in uncomfortable conversations — we are already living with awareness. We are already alive.

From there, we can explore spirituality, success, or purpose. But now, we will be choosing those paths from a place of strength, not from a place of escape.

In the next chapter, we'll look at one of the biggest ways we hide this truth: through **pleasant-sounding talk** that keeps us smiling on the outside while shrinking on the inside.

The Smoke Screen of Goody-Goody Talk

Wherever we go – a wedding, a workplace, a café, or even a WhatsApp group – we try to keep things light and pleasant. We crack easy jokes, give compliments, and avoid tension.

It's a habit many of us carry. We want to be liked, seen as kind, and easy to be around – so we speak in a way that feels safe, even if it isn't always honest.

In Indian families, this pattern is even more common. When we meet relatives, we follow a set way of speaking – full of warm words, polite smiles, and predictable conversations. This behaviour is often done out of respect and tradition. Even if something feels off, we tend to ignore it. We avoid serious talks. We keep emotions in check. The priority becomes keeping the surface smooth, even if things under the surface are not.

You might be sitting with a group of friends, and someone makes a comment that feels off. Maybe it's a joke that targets someone or an opinion you don't agree with. But instead of saying anything, everyone just laughs, nods, and moves on. The mood stays cheerful, the smiles stay on, and no one brings up the discomfort. Everything looks perfectly fine on the surface, even though something small didn't feel right.

Now, it's not wrong to be pleasant. Infect being kind and respectful should be the way to talk to people. But the problem begins when this becomes the only way we know how to talk — when every conversation becomes about sounding good, staying agreeable, and avoiding anything that might be uncomfortable. Slowly, we forget how to be real with each other. The need to keep things "nice" starts killing the space for truth.

Once this becomes the norm, people start feeling stuck. They begin to carry silent pressure — to smile when they're hurt, to agree when they want to say no, to laugh when they don't even feel present. They feel something inside but don't know how to express it. And the more they hold back, the more disconnected they feel — not just from others, but from themselves.

Over time, this habit of goody-goody talk creates emotional distance. People start feeling alone even in groups. They don't feel truly seen or heard. And worst of all, they start thinking that their real feelings are wrong. They begin to believe that being honest will ruin relationships or invite judgment. So they keep everything inside and carry a quiet sadness that no one notices.

This way of speaking may look peaceful on the outside, but inside, it often hides tension, hesitation, and fear — the fear of being misunderstood, the fear of being seen as difficult, the fear of losing connection. And because everyone is wearing the same mask, no one makes the first move to drop it.

But real connection only happens when we are real — when we stop performing and start sharing what we actually feel. This doesn't mean we stop being respectful. It just means we give space to honesty too. A simple sentence like "I feel different" or "I'm not okay today" can open doors that surface talk never will.

Let's not throw away sweetness. Let's just not let it hide everything else. Because underneath the polite words, most people are craving one thing – **realness**. And maybe, it starts with us.

In the next chapter, we'll see how this shrinking isn't limited to one group of people. Whether rich or poor, loud or quiet, almost everyone carries this hidden emotional suffering – they've just learned different ways to hide it.

The Hidden Suffering Across All Economic Classes

It is often assumed that deep emotional suffering is mostly found in people with fewer resources – those struggling to make ends meet, living in cramped spaces, or dealing with the visible hardships of poverty. It's easy to believe that the pain of feeling small, ignored, or left out belongs only to the lower or lower-middle classes. But this is far from the full picture.

I have met families with huge houses, two cars, and weekend parties – and still found the same silent hurt sitting at their dining tables. They wear new clothes, speak good English, and travel abroad. Yet when they gather, some voices stay small, some smiles hide fear, and someone always feels pushed aside. Money does not erase this.

Why? Because the real problem is not in the wallet; it is in the way people share space every day. The moment two or more humans meet – at work, at school, in a park, or on a video call – an invisible game begins:

Who will lead? Who will listen? Who will adjust?

That game plays out in every class, from a village tea stall to a billionaire's boardroom.

Think of an elite dinner. Everyone there is "successful." Still, you will spot one person talking over others, another laughing on cue, and a third one staring at the floor, counting minutes. The labels of rich or poor disappear. What matters is **relative power in that moment** — who dares to speak and who swallows their words.

The same pattern repeats in the middle class. A group of colleagues meets after office hours. They all earn similar salaries, yet one dominates the plan for the weekend. The quiet ones nod, even when they dislike the idea. Later, they go home feeling small, wondering why they couldn't object. The pain is the same; only the backdrop changes.

Lower-income groups face it too. In a workers' hostel, ten men share one room. One of them controls the TV remote. Another decides when the lights go off. The rest keep adjusting. Again, money is not the root; the **structure of interaction** is.

So let us drop the myth that wealth protects people from this suffering. It does not.

The fear of losing respect, the urge to keep peace, and the wish to save face — all these live in every human heart. Wherever there is a group, the dance of dominance and silence starts.

Why does this pain appear in every group?

- **Unspoken group roles.** In most group settings, people naturally fall into roles — some lead, some follow, and some stay quiet. These roles aren't always chosen; they often just happen. And when your natural voice doesn't match the role you've been pushed into, suffering begins.

- **Fear of disapproval.** Whether you're sitting in a boardroom or on a plastic stool by a tea stall, the fear of being judged, dismissed, or excluded stops people from expressing what they truly feel.
- **Emotional unpreparedness.** We were rarely taught how to stay centered when feeling ignored or overpowered. So we either shrink or fight back in ways that don't help. Both responses come from pain, and neither truly solves it.

Economic layers are like different stages in a theatre. The costumes change, the set changes, but the script of silent suffering can stay the same.

Once we understand this, we stop envying those above us and stop looking down on those below.

We start focusing on the real work — learning to hold our ground, speak our truth, and let others do the same, no matter what the bank balance says.

Distorted Perception of Being Kind and Good-Hearted

When people are unable to handle disagreement, awkward moments, or indirect conversations, they gradually lose their personal space and voice. Over time, they start feeling like things are being done **to** them. This gives rise to a deep pain in the heart — a subtle, constant suffering that's hard to explain.

In an attempt to process this pain, they share their experience with close friends or loved ones. And through those discussions, they find comfort in a familiar explanation:

They were exploited because they were "kind" and "good-hearted."

That's why we frequently hear this narrative — that the world is cruel, that bad people take advantage, and that good people always end up suffering. It's a story that sounds noble, but it can be misleading.

Let's look at this with more honesty:

More often than not, we weren't victims because we were too kind — we were victims because we lacked the ability to assert ourselves in difficult moments. The other person was just smarter, quicker, or more emotionally resilient.

And yes — the "victim" in this case is not always as noble as the story suggests.

This illusion — that goodness and kindness naturally attract suffering — is a dangerous belief. It makes people **fear kindness.** It makes them believe that they must become harsh or unkind in order to protect themselves.

But in reality, **kindness isn't weakness.** It just needs to be paired with **clarity**, **strength**, and **presence**.

Let's try to understand the true meaning of **kindness** and being **good-hearted**.

A truly kind person is someone who **has the power to hurt others** but **chooses not to**. They have the strength to cause suffering but still act with compassion and respect. That's what it really means to be **good-hearted**.

On the other hand, if someone is simply **incapable** of standing up for themselves or taking action, and they suffer in silence, that is **not kindness**. That is **incompetence** or **powerlessness**, not a moral choice.

Let's look at this from another perspective — **forgiveness**.

Imagine a poor man is abused by a powerful man. The poor man cannot do anything in return. He is angry and helpless. One day, he reads a quote that says, *"Don't hold grudges, forgive those who hurt you."* Inspired by this, he decides to forgive the powerful man and tells everyone how forgiving he is.

But is that real forgiveness?

Not really. That's just a way of **covering his helplessness**. He had no choice but to accept what happened. Calling it "forgiveness" doesn't make it genuine.

Now imagine a different situation. A powerful man is insulted or hurt by someone. He has the resources, position, and strength to ruin that person's life — but he **chooses not to**. He consciously decides to let go and move on. That is **real forgiveness**.

True **kindness** and being **good-hearted** come from a place of strength. It means you are **able to hold your ground**, **assert yourself**, and **take charge of your life** — and still choose to respect others, honor their dignity, and allow them space to speak.

No one taught us to protect our 'Emotional Space'

School teaches how to solve math problems, write essays, memorize facts, and pass exams. We're taught how to calculate, how to compete, and how to perform. But in all those years, no one really teaches us how to protect something very important — our **personal space**.

And its not about physical space.

We're talking about **emotional space** — the right to be heard, the right to say "no," the right to exist fully in a conversation without shrinking.

We are never formally taught how to hold our ground without guilt, how to stay calm when someone oversteps, or how to express discomfort without sounding rude. These things are left to luck. If someone learns it, they learn it by accident — through pain, mistakes, or survival.

From childhood, we are trained to adjust. Be obedient. Be respectful. Don't question elders. Don't speak too much. Say yes, even if it means saying no to yourself.

And slowly, without even noticing, we learn that **keeping peace is more important than keeping ourselves.**

This becomes our default setting. And by the time we grow up, we don't even realise that we've lost the basic ability to say:

"I'm not okay with this."

There's no school class for this. No exam. No textbook that says:

"Here's what to do when you feel small in a room full of loud voices."

We are left to figure it out on our own. And when we fail — when we stay silent, when we freeze, when we overthink — we blame ourselves.

We think we're weak. We think something is wrong with us.

But the truth is — **no one trained us.**

What makes it even harder is this: some people seem to be naturally good at holding their space. They speak clearly. They say "no" easily. They don't get affected much by people's opinions. And it looks like they've figured it out.

But even they didn't learn it in a formal way. It's not like they took a class or read a guidebook. They just somehow built that attitude — maybe from their environment, maybe their personality, maybe luck. It's all random and this randomness makes things even more confusing for the rest of us.

We look at them and wonder, **"Why can't I be like that?"**

We feel left behind.

But the truth is, this is not about intelligence or talent — **this is about emotional training**, and most of us never got it.

This silence around emotional space becomes a blind spot in our entire society. Nobody talks about it, so nobody even knows they need it. That's why people confuse being "good" with being quiet. They confuse being "kind" with being invisible. They think being respected means not creating any discomfort — even if that discomfort is real and necessary.

If we had formal emotional education, we would know how to notice discomfort instead of ignoring it.

We would know how to draw boundaries with grace.

We would know how to listen without losing ourselves.

But since we didn't learn any of this, we carry fear.

We carry guilt.

And we try to survive moments by either staying quiet, pleasing others, or suddenly exploding when it gets too much.

This book itself is an attempt to give that missing education — to name the experiences we all go through but never talk about.

And more than giving answers, it hopes to bring awareness — that you were never broken, you were just **never taught**.

Bad Habit of Directly Jumping to Solutions

Whenever someone faces an emotional struggle, the most common thing they say is,

"Just tell me what to do."

People want quick solutions. They want a ready-made trick or a simple method that will take away the discomfort immediately. They expect a few clear steps, like a recipe – something they can apply straight away, and everything will become okay again.

But this habit of directly jumping to the solution is where the real problem begins.

It looks practical from the outside, but deep down, it's an escape.

It's our mind trying to run away from the discomfort instead of understanding it.

We feel the pain for a few seconds and immediately ask,

"How do I fix this?"

We don't even take time to see what exactly is happening –

Where is it coming from?

Why does it keep repeating?

How are we reacting to it?

We just want to move past it — without truly facing it.

This way of dealing with things creates a very shallow kind of growth. You may feel better for a while, but soon you'll get stuck again — because the root pattern is still inside you. The problem will come back in a different form, and again you'll go looking for another shortcut.

This loop continues because we never actually understand the full depth of what we're going through.

Another issue is that people usually only see their own kind of pain.

Someone might say, "I just want to learn how to say no,"

while someone else may say, "I freeze in awkward moments."

But most of the time, we are carrying multiple layers of suffering — not just one.

We just don't see them all clearly.

Sometimes, you may be suffering in one area but unaware of three other patterns silently working in the background.

That's why — before talking about what to do — we need to take a pause and look at the entire picture.

Let's not rush into fixing things right away.

Let's not beg for answers before we've even understood the questions.

Because without this clarity, even the best advice will fall flat.

So, here's what I invite you to do –

Let's go through this journey together, one step at a time.

Let's take some space and courage to see the different types of emotional pain we experience –

Not just the ones we're aware of, but even those that quietly shape our reactions and choices every day.

Let's observe them – without panic, without judgment.

In the next few chap

Scared to Disagree

This happens to most of us — more frequent than we admit.

Whether we're in a team meeting at work, sitting with friends at a party, or chatting with family over dinner — there comes a moment when someone says something off. Maybe it's an ignorant comment, maybe it's a half-truth, or maybe it's just plain wrong.

But still, we stay quiet.

We pause.

We hesitate.

A few dominant — or let's just say loud — voices tend to take over the conversation. Their opinions start sounding like facts, simply because no one is challenging them.

And the rest of us?

We go into silent mode.

Even if we strongly disagree inside, we smile, nod, or change the topic.

Anything but confrontation.

Why We Fear Disagreement

- **We're taught disagreement is disrespect.**
  - ✓ From a young age, we've been told to "not talk back," "listen to elders," and "avoid arguments." Somewhere along the way, disagreement started to feel like being rude.
- **We don't want to create awkwardness.**
  - ✓ Speaking up means making the atmosphere tense – and most of us are conditioned to avoid any discomfort in social settings.
- **We fear being judged.**
  - ✓ What if they think I'm arrogant? Or aggressive? Or trying to "show off"?
  - ✓ This fear makes us hold back even when we know we should speak.
- **We fear breaking the harmony.**
  - ✓ In families, friend circles, or teams – we want to maintain peace. Disagreement feels like inviting chaos.
- **We're afraid of losing connection.**
  - ✓ Deep down, we fear that one disagreement could harm the relationship.
  - ✓ So we choose silence over risk.

What It Leads To

- **Unspoken resentment builds up.**
  - ✓ Each time we don't express ourselves, we carry the discomfort longer than we should.
- **We slowly lose confidence.**
  - ✓ Constant silence in moments that matter sends a message to our own mind:
  - ✓ **"Your voice doesn't matter."**
- **Dominant voices remain unchecked.**
  - ✓ When no one disagrees, people start believing their opinion is the ultimate truth.
- **Honest conversations disappear.**
  - ✓ Everyone wears a mask of agreement. Real issues never get addressed.
- **We stop trusting ourselves.**
  - ✓ The more we ignore our inner voice, the more disconnected we feel from who we really are.

But here's the truth:

Disagreement is not disrespect.

Disagreement – when expressed with calm and clarity – is a sign that you're thinking.

That you care enough to engage and you're present in the moment, not just nodding to please people. It's not about creating conflict, it's about **contributing.**

Think about it – how do ideas improve?

How does society grow?

Through debates. Through opposing views. Through questions that push the boundaries of what we already know.

Disagreement is not a disruption – it's a **driving force for growth.**

Still, it's hard.

The moment you say, "I don't agree with that," all eyes turn to you.

You feel exposed.

You wonder if you've made things uncomfortable.

You start second-guessing yourself.

It's even harder when the person you're disagreeing with is older, more respected, or always sounds confident. Challenging them feels like breaking a social contract.

So, once again, you let it go.

But every time we let it go, we shrink a little inside.

We carry that sense of compromise.

That feeling of "I didn't show up for myself."

And that feeling stays.

Guilt and Fear of Saying 'No'

Saying "No" is actually a subset of disagreement – but it's not always seen that way.

When someone asks for a favour or expects your time, effort, or money, you may genuinely want to help.

But what happens when you're not in a position to do so?

More often than not, **you still say "Yes."**

Not because you want to – but because you simply couldn't say "No."

You feel guilty.

You feel afraid.

And you end up doing something **against your will.**

In that moment, you become the victim – even if no one else realizes it.

You sacrificed your comfort, time, or resources – not out of love or generosity, but because you couldn't refuse.

That's a very different feeling.

Saying "No" sounds simple in theory.

We hear things like "You should have boundaries" or "Be confident in your choices."

But the real emotion of saying "No" to someone – especially someone who has been nice to you – is incredibly uncomfortable.

You start imagining their reaction before even saying the word:

- *What if they feel bad?*
- *What if they think I'm selfish?*
- *What if this creates a conflict?*
- *What if I need their help later?*

Even in formal or surface-level relationships – where you hardly know each other – you may feel that pressure.

Say someone from work or your extended social circle suddenly calls and asks for a loan.

You weren't close, and you're not in a position to help – but you still say yes, just to avoid the awkwardness of refusal.

It's not just about money. This fear of saying "No" shows up everywhere:

- When someone asks you to stay back for extra work
- When a relative expects you to attend an event
- When a friend wants something that makes you uncomfortable

There's also a parallel fear:

Even when you're firm in your refusal, a voice inside says:

"What if I need their help in the future?"

This voice is not always wrong — but it makes you operate from fear, not clarity.

And when fear is the base of your decisions, you will always feel unsettled.

Saying "No" — **firmly and kindly** — is one of the hardest emotional muscles to build.

But it's also one of the most essential if you want to live life on your terms.

The Fear of Facing Awkward Moments

We all have experienced situations where awkward moments happen – moments that feel tight, strange, and very uncomfortable. People become uneasy, unsettled, and they try to end the awkwardness as quickly as possible, almost like escaping from danger.

Once, me and three other friends went to a restaurant. We had a good time, laughed, and enjoyed the food. But when we reached the billing counter, everything changed. No one was saying anything, and a strange silence took over. Who's going to pay the bill? That one question silently floated in the air – and no one was ready to ask it directly. The tension kept building. And finally, one of the friends – who probably couldn't handle the awkwardness anymore – quickly paid the bill, just to end the discomfort.

This may sound small, but if you're from India or even have a similar culture, you'll know how common this is. When friends go shopping, go to a café, or order something online – this invisible pressure always shows up. And the person who is most afraid of awkwardness often ends up paying the money. Not because they wanted to, not because they were being generous – but because they wanted to escape that weird silence.

It's very hard to deal with these moments. I'm not going to sit here and give big advice like "do this" or "say that." Because honestly, I've suffered a lot because of this too.

Even now, sometimes I feel that same tightness in my chest when something gets awkward. My hands sweat. My mind starts racing with thoughts like "What should I say?" "What if I look cheap?" "Will they judge me?" "Should I offer? Should I not?" All this confusion, just because I can't sit with a little discomfort.

And that's the real problem — we're not trained to sit with uncomfortable moments. No one teaches us how to deal with them. We are taught to be polite, nice, and well-mannered — but no one prepares us for real-life social tension. So when it happens, we either freeze or do something that goes against our own comfort.

You know what's worse? After the moment is over — after you've paid the bill or said "yes" just to avoid tension — you don't feel happy. You feel cheated. You feel like you betrayed yourself. And then you overthink it for hours, maybe even days, trying to make sense of what just happened.

The problem isn't just the moment. It's the weight of the moment. The fear of how you'll be perceived. The guilt of saying something honest. The discomfort of not knowing how the other person will react.

And that's why we run away.

Some people avoid meetups altogether. Some people become over-generous — not from the heart, but just to avoid any possible friction. Some become overly silent or passive, so they don't have to deal with tricky conversations. But deep down, they're just afraid of one thing – awkwardness.

Here's the thing: awkwardness is not always a bad sign. In fact, it often means that something real is happening. Something that doesn't follow the script. And that's where real connections, real honesty, and real growth start.

So instead of always trying to end the awkward moment, maybe we can try to pause and stay in it for just a few seconds longer. Just enough to remind ourselves: "It's okay. This will pass." You don't have to solve everything immediately. You don't have to speak perfectly. You don't have to pay the bill every time just to avoid tension.

It's not easy. But slowly, moment by moment, we can train ourselves to be comfortable in the uncomfortable.

And once you learn to face awkwardness without panic – you take back a part of your power.

Not Able to Tackle Indirect Conversations

I hope everyone understands what indirect conversations are. These are those slippery exchanges where someone says something with a hidden motive — but frames it in such a way that if you try to point out the real intention, they can easily deny it. In fact, it can backfire on you. You might end up being blamed for "overthinking" or "being too sensitive."

I'm honestly the worst when it comes to handling this. Whenever someone talks to me indirectly, I get very uneasy. I become restless inside. My mind starts racing — "Did they really mean that?" "Should I respond or just stay quiet?" I start doubting myself. And when I try to do indirect conversation myself, it's even worse. I feel weak, exposed, and anxious — as if the other person can see through everything I'm trying to say and is just quietly watching me fumble.

That's the thing: indirect conversation messes with your head. There's a strange power imbalance built into it. The person using it always has the upper hand, because they're hiding their real intent behind layers. You, on the other hand, are stuck between silence and risk. If you respond directly, they can simply say, "I didn't mean that," or "You're reading too much into it." But if you stay quiet, you feel like you've surrendered.

So yes, both doing indirect conversation and handling it are important. Because life forces you into these situations, whether you like it or not.

But here's what I've learned — handling indirect conversations is not about clever replies or being cunning. It requires a mix of emotional intelligence, calmness, and a bit of distance. You need to stay aware of what's really happening underneath the words, without reacting impulsively. And that's not easy.

People who are innocent, kind-hearted, or naturally introverted — these are the ones who suffer the most here. They don't want to play games. They want to speak clearly, live honestly. But this world isn't always that straightforward. So they either stay quiet and keep absorbing the discomfort, or they speak up and get told they're "too sensitive."

And then the loop begins.

They walk away from that conversation, but it doesn't end there. It stays with them. They keep thinking, "Why did I freeze?" "I should've said this instead." They replay the entire conversation in their head again and again — looking for that one perfect sentence that could've fixed everything.

But it never comes.

Sometimes I feel like people who talk indirectly are never fully honest — even with themselves. They throw subtle comments, vague lines, and carefully designed sentences to test your reaction. And if you catch it? They escape. If you miss it? They win. That's the mental game going on.

And what makes it worse is that it looks harmless from the outside. To anyone watching, the conversation looks normal. Nothing aggressive, nothing openly insulting. But inside, you're feeling all kinds of things – hurt, confused, frustrated.

That's the real trap of indirect communication. It affects you, but you can't explain why it affected you. You just know something was off.

And this trap slowly makes you doubt your own perception.

You begin to wonder if maybe you're just too sensitive… maybe you're overreacting. And once that self-doubt creeps in, it becomes even harder to respond the next time.

We'll discuss practical ways to handle this in a later chapter. For now, just understand – indirect communication is a deeply complex pattern. And it silently steals your clarity, peace, and emotional energy if you don't learn how to handle it.

You Need Ground, Not Enlightenment

No spirituality, no philosopher, and no motivational speaker can actually give you the real solution for this.

Yes, they will talk about "higher paths," "letting go," "being mindful," and "finding peace" — but all that is just talk. **Goody-goody ways. Nothing more.**

They can never feel the pain, the awkwardness, or the anxiety that you're going through.

They don't know what it feels like when your chest tightens in a tough conversation.

They don't know the guilt that comes when you say "No" to someone and feel like you've done something wrong.

And still, they keep giving lectures as if they are some kinds of supreme entity who has figured everything out.

They speak, but they don't feel.

I've seen it many times — in spiritual programs or motivational talks — the major part of the crowd is made up of people who are mentally drained, emotionally weak, and are constantly running away from their real problems.

They just want to feel better — even if it's temporary.

And that comfort comes from hearing things like:

- "You are not the body, you are the soul."
- "This world is temporary."
- "Material things don't matter."
- "Rich people are not happy either."

These lines sound deep, but they don't help when you're stuck in real life.

When someone crosses your boundary and you can't say anything — what use is a soul talk at that moment?

Sometimes, I really don't get it.

Why do these spiritual gurus, philosophers, and motivational speakers behave as if they have the ownership of happiness? As if everyone else is lost, and only they know the truth?

In reality none of them can sit in your discomfort.

None of them will stand with you when you're sweating in silence, unable to respond.

None of them will help you when you are overthinking for hours after one small conversation.

They don't have to go through what you are going through.

And still, they act as if they can guide you.

This is your journey.

That's why I say —

Only you know how it feels.

Only you know how hard it is.

The First Time I Spoke My Truth

It had been around two years since I completed graduation and started working as a software engineer in an MNC. Life was kind of on track – regular job, decent friends, and that phase where you're figuring out adulthood one small moment at a time.

It was my birthday, and I thought of inviting a few colleagues to my flat. It was a simple 2 BHK setup – one room was mine, and the other belonged to my flatmate. I didn't plan anything big, just a few drinks and casual conversation. Some colleagues were of the same age, some were seniors, and everyone seemed happy to come.

By evening, everyone arrived. The mood was light. We were chilling, laughing, talking about random things. There was nothing extraordinary about it – just one of those "feel-good" house gatherings.

During the flow of the evening, one of my senior colleagues said something casually like, "I'll stay back here tonight, I'll leave tomorrow."

Without thinking too much, I just said, "Okay." It was said in a relaxed tone, and I also responded in that relaxed mood. I didn't process the meaning fully at that moment.

Later, the gathering ended, and people started leaving one by one. Slowly, the house became quiet. The music was off, the plates were cleared, and the leftover glasses were lying around. Everyone had gone – except that one senior colleague. He had casually changed into more comfortable clothes and was sitting in the room.

That's when something started feeling heavy in me.

I remembered I actually had some other plans for the night – plans that I couldn't go ahead with if someone was staying over. My mind started racing, but I couldn't say anything. I kept moving around the house, cleaning a bit, trying to act normal, but inside I was extremely uncomfortable.

It was a strange state. He hadn't done anything wrong. He had spoken nicely throughout. But now the situation was out of sync with what I truly wanted.

I kept walking from one corner of the flat to another, trying to calm my body down. My chest was tight. My head was spinning with questions like –

"What if he feels offended?"

"Will this affect our office relation?"

"Am I being rude?"

But under all of that, there was one clear voice inside me:

"I want him to leave. I want my space tonight."

But saying that… to a senior… after already agreeing once… felt like a mountain.

I stepped outside the flat into the corridor and just stood there.

I didn't know what I was waiting for — maybe for courage to appear magically.

I stood for almost five minutes, playing different versions of the conversation in my head.

Each one made my hands shake even more.

But then a new thought came —

If I don't speak now, I won't sleep peacefully. I'll stay angry with myself. I'll feel small again.

And I had done that too many times already.

So I finally decided — no matter how awkward this is going to be, I'll say it.

I walked back in.

He was sitting in the room, relaxed, checking his phone.

I stood at the door, looked at him, and said slowly,

"Hey… this may sound odd. It was my mistake that I didn't say it earlier, but I actually have other plans tonight. So I want to tell you — you'll have to leave now."

It was a silent moment. Our eyes met.

For a few seconds, neither of us spoke — just looked at each other. The room felt strangely still, like everything had paused.

There was a heat in my ears, a kind of ringing silence in the background.

My chest was tight, my thoughts completely blank.

It was one of those moments where your body knows it's a big deal, even before your mind can explain why.

Then, holding that heaviness in the air, I finally continued,

"I'm not able to handle my emotions right now… it's feeling too heavy inside. I'm going to step out of the flat. Please change back and come outside. I'll wait at the gate."

And I left.

My heart was pounding. I didn't even know what kind of expression I had while saying those words.

My face was probably red, and I was breathing fast.

But I felt one thing clearly — **I had said what I truly felt.**

After about 5–7 minutes, he came out.

He had changed back into his clothes.

He looked at me and laughed a little —

"You could've told me earlier, man."

He said it lightly, not with anger.

Then he picked up his bike keys, smiled, and left.

The next day in office, I was still unsure how he'd behave with me.

But to my surprise, he was warm, normal — even cheerful.

He said he was actually glad that I expressed what I really felt.

And that stayed with me.

This may look small from the outside. But for me, it was massive.

I had always imagined that protecting your space means conflict, drama, or guilt.

But sometimes, it just means standing in one hard moment and telling the truth – even if your voice is shaking.

I didn't win an argument that day.

I won something deeper – my own respect.

You Must Take It Seriously First.

So far, we've discussed, analyzed, and deeply felt a common pain — the pain of silently suffering.

We live in a country that's free. Every citizen is free to live the way they want, to pursue their dreams, and to chart their own path. But when it comes to **emotional freedom**, that's a different story altogether.

In the emotional world, most of us are **slaves**, caught in chains we don't even see. These chains aren't physical — they're emotional. They imprison our **voice**, our **presence**, and our ability to fully exist in the world. Emotional slavery isn't something you can see from the outside.

It's the quiet, invisible pain of being unable to express, to stand tall, or to fully claim your space — even among people who love you.

You can't escape it. You can't run away. You can't even confront it properly.

It's as if everything is happening in front of your eyes, and you remain helpless. That, to me, is the greatest kind of pain — invisible to others, yet deeply wounding from within.

So... What Now?

Are we just going to sit with the pain and keep analysing it endlessly? Or are we going to **do something** about it?

To begin changing, we first need to decode the structure of this emotional slavery. There are **four essential steps** that can help us overcome it:

1. Developing **seriousness** to truly want to break free
2. People on the other side are not 'Gifted'
3. Building the **courage to feel and embrace** uncomfortable emotions
4. Being **ready to be misunderstood** at the start

This chapter is about the **first and most important step**: **seriousness**.

The next three will be explored in the following chapters.

Let's start with -

Seriousness to Overcome Emotional Slavery

Often, when we open up about these emotional struggles, people around us respond with dismissal:

"Why are you taking this so seriously?"

"Everyone goes through this."

"It's nothing – just let it go."

We're made to feel like our pain isn't valid. That it's an overreaction. That we're being too sensitive.

But for some of us, it's not just a passing discomfort – it's something that affects us deeply.

It stays in our chest. It follows us home. It makes us question ourselves long after the moment has passed.

So let me be clear:

If you're someone for whom these feelings seem minor, or you find it easy to move on from them – this book may not speak to you deeply. And that's okay. No judgment. We're all built differently.

But if you're someone who gets **emotionally disturbed** when your space is crossed,

If you **carry discomfort** inside you for days,

If you keep replaying moments when you couldn't speak up,

If those silences feel like **self-betrayal**...

Then this book is for **you**.

I am that kind of person too.

And for people like us, this isn't about personality. It's about **respecting what hurts us**, and finally doing something about it.

This kind of emotional pain isn't small. It's not dramatic. It's real.

And the only way to work through it is to take it **seriously**.

Without seriousness, no solution will stick.

No method will work.

Because the moment discomfort returns, you'll retreat – unless you've truly committed to changing how you respond.

So before moving to the next chapter, ask yourself:

- Do I really want to change how I handle emotional discomfort?
- Am I willing to sit with what I've avoided?
- Can I stop calling my pain "small" and start treating it like it matters?

If your answer is yes — then you're ready for the real work.

In the next chapter, we'll talk about something even more important:

The courage to feel what you've been avoiding.

But none of that will matter...if you don't take this part — your beginning — seriously.

People on the Other Side Are Not 'Gifted'

There is an assumption, or you can say a quiet belief, that people who are emotionally strong – the ones who can easily hold their ground, speak without fear, or say "no" without guilt – must be gifted in some way. When we see these people in action, when we observe how calmly they disagree, how they don't freeze in awkward moments, and how they protect their space without hesitation, we start to feel that they have something special.

We admire them. We even start to genuinely respect them – not just for what they say, but for how naturally and effortlessly they seem to handle emotionally difficult situations. In our mind, they start to feel like they are one step above us, especially when it comes to emotional authority or presence.

We assume that either life has taught them something we missed, or they are just built differently. Maybe they had to face tough situations in life that trained them emotionally. Or maybe their emotional structure is simply such that they don't experience the same discomfort that we do. They don't freeze up. They don't get lost in fear. They don't overthink after speaking up. And because we know how tough it is to protect our emotional space, we don't even envy them. Instead, we quietly put ourselves in the position of a follower.

We believe we are not made like that. We start living with the idea that maybe leadership — emotional or otherwise — is not for people like us. And even though a part of us dreams of being like them, of owning space and speaking clearly, we just keep adjusting and surviving.

But let me tell you something clearly — and I mean this with full honesty: the people on the other side are not gifted at all. The only thing they are "gifted" with is that they don't suffer as much from uncomfortable emotions in those moments. That's the only real difference.

When people like us try to hold the ground, we feel a rush of uneasy emotions. We may go blank, feel guilty, or even freeze. But when they do the same thing, they usually don't panic. Their minds stay steady. Their bodies don't shake. Their voice doesn't tremble. The act may be the same — speaking, disagreeing, drawing boundaries — but the emotional experience is completely different.

That difference in emotional appearance is what tricks us. They seem calm, while we struggle to remain steady. They stay in control, while we internally feel like a mess. But in reality, both are doing the same thing — asserting themselves. And just because someone else does it with less emotional noise doesn't mean they are better or more meant for it. It just means their nervous system doesn't panic like ours does. That's it.

In fact, people on the other side might even feel proud about how calm and composed they were. And that's okay. Let them feel that way. But we don't need to compare ourselves to them in that moment. **Because our focus is not to win a contest in stillness. Our focus is to hold the ground — and we did**. Maybe we spoke with a trembling voice. Maybe our hands were sweating. Maybe we didn't look strong. But we were strong. Because we didn't back down. We didn't collapse into silence. We stayed. And we said what needed to be said.

It's important to understand that not feeling fear doesn't make someone stronger. Strength is when you move forward even with the fear still present inside you. Just because someone looks emotionally polished doesn't mean they have more value than you.

The shaking voice that still speaks has more honesty than the steady voice that's only used to stay in control. You may not feel smooth or confident yet. You may feel clumsy or emotionally overwhelmed while doing what's right for you. But none of that makes your effort less valuable.

So the next time you admire someone who seems emotionally stronger than you, don't forget to see your own effort clearly. Don't let their smooth appearance make you feel like you're failing. You're not. You are learning to do the same thing — just from a different starting point. You are not behind. You are not broken. You are not less. You are simply in training. And every step you take, even the shaky ones, counts.

Courage to Embrace and Feel the Raw, Uncomfortable Emotions

Let's now talk about something very important – something that actually stops us from speaking up and claiming our space.

Many times in life, we go through situations where we cannot stand up for ourselves. We want to speak, we want to take space, but we fail to do so. And later, we feel like a victim. We wonder why we went silent. We feel small, helpless, or even angry at ourselves.

From the outside, it looks simple – just speak, just say what you want. Just raise your voice or put your point across. It doesn't seem like a big task. But the real problem doesn't start with the act of speaking. The real struggle begins with the emotions that rise just before we try to speak.

These emotions make everything difficult. They confuse us, make us shaky, and create fear inside. When we try to express ourselves, these emotions take over and make us feel weak, nervous, or scared. They make us feel so uncomfortable that we often give up on the moment. We choose to stay quiet, just to avoid the emotional mess that follows.

What makes it even more difficult is that these emotions don't come one by one. They come like a wave – fast and strong. One emotion brings another, and soon you are caught in a chain of feelings. Fear turns into shame. Shame turns into helplessness. Helplessness turns into anger. And suddenly, you feel like escaping the situation altogether.

Sometimes, the emotions are so powerful that even the other person in the room starts to feel uncomfortable. They may not understand what is going on, but they sense the tension. This makes the situation awkward for both sides.

Let me share something funny but true about myself. Sometimes I go on YouTube and watch videos of awkward moments – scenes from Bollywood, politics, or interviews. When I see those moments where people don't know how to react, I start feeling uncomfortable myself. Even though I'm just watching a video on my phone or laptop, I feel so awkward that I have to stop the video. I close it because I cannot bear to watch what's happening. That's how strong these emotions can be – even when they are happening to someone else on a screen.

So imagine how intense it must be when you are actually in that situation – when you are the one living it. These raw emotions take full control of your body and mind. And if we don't learn how to deal with them, we will always stay silent. We will always back down.

If we really want to come out of emotional slavery, we must stop running from these emotions. We must start learning how to face them. We must build the courage to feel them – fully and honestly.

We need to allow these emotions to pass through us instead of pushing them away. Yes, they will make you feel uncomfortable. Yes, they might make your body react in strange ways. But if you stay with them long enough, they pass. And when they pass, something inside you grows stronger.

Here are some examples of how these emotions may show up:

You may feel that your body becomes stiff or your hands start shaking.

You may not be able to speak clearly or finish a sentence properly.

You may fumble or go blank.

You may feel heat in your ears or a tightness in your chest.

You may even hear someone in the room say something sarcastic like, "Look at this guy, trying to act smart."

That one comment can make you want to disappear. But if you choose to stay — if you let the emotion move through you — you will see that after a few minutes, it starts to fade.

This is what emotional strength really is. Not the ability to talk loudly. Not the ability to argue well. But the ability to stand inside an uncomfortable emotion and not run away.

In fact, people's emotional strength can be measured by how much discomfort they can tolerate. How much awkwardness can they handle before shutting down?

How many seconds of silence or tension can they survive before giving up?

That's what truly separates strong people from the rest.

If we want to grow, if we want to claim our emotional freedom, then this is the kind of strength we need to build. Not all at once. Not in one day. But slowly — by allowing yourself to feel uncomfortable without panicking.

You don't have to handle everything perfectly. You don't have to respond cleverly every time. You just have to stay with the emotion for a few more seconds than you did last time. Let it rise. Let it pass. And soon, you will see that the fear you had was not as big as it felt.

This is how emotional slavery breaks. Not with one big action, but with small acts of courage — the courage to feel.

And once you learn to feel, you start learning how to heal.

Being Misunderstood Is Part of the Process

We've already come a long way in understanding ourselves. And one thing is clear now: if we really want to grow, we have to face those difficult emotions we've been running from. There's no other way around it. You'll have to stand in the middle of that discomfort—whether it's anxiety, fear, hesitation, or awkwardness. Those emotions are not signs of weakness; they are signs that you're finally doing something real.

But just when you're ready to go through all this, another challenge quietly shows up. It doesn't feel like a big deal at first, but it can stop you right there. It's the need to be understood.

You start thinking, *"**I hope they know I'm not being rude or negative. I'm just doing this to protect my space.**"* You want people to see your side, to understand your intention, and to know that you're still a good person.

This feeling seems harmless, but it can become a dangerous block in your path.

Because once again, your focus shifts from doing what's right for you... to making sure others are comfortable with what you're doing.

Now think about someone who has always stayed silent, who's never stood up for himself before. If that person finally decides to speak up and take space, how do you think people around them will react?

Of course, it might come across as "wrong" at first.

People are not used to this new version of you. They've gotten used to the quiet one, the adjusting one. So when you suddenly say something strong, when you protect your space, it may surprise them. Some might even say weird things like, *"Why are you acting like this now?"* or *"You've changed."*

And in that moment, you might feel hurt. But don't let it stop you.

If you keep going—if you stay consistent—something powerful happens.

With time, the same people who questioned your voice will start respecting it.

They'll adjust. They'll understand.

Your strength will slowly become part of your identity in their eyes too.

There's also another fear that comes up. A heavy one.

You may think, *"What if I start voicing my feelings, and in the process, I lose people? What if I end up all alone?"*

That fear is very real. But here's what you need to hold on to:

Even if you do lose a few people, **saving your own voice and space is still more important** than the pain of being alone.

And here's the surprising part: most of this fear is just imagination.

In reality, people usually don't run away. Many of them are going through the exact same struggle.

They've also been quietly hurting, adjusting, and feeling unseen.

So when they see you speak up, they feel inspired. They feel connected.

Some of them will come closer to you—not leave.

They'll respect you more. Some will become even better friends than before.

So let's bring all of this together.

First, we've understood that the only way to real growth is by facing those uneasy emotions head-on.

Second, we need to let go of the need to always be understood. That urge can quietly pull us backward.

Third, it's natural that people will take time to adjust to the new, more honest version of you. They may not get it at first, but they will with time.

And lastly, we need to be okay with the possibility that some people may walk away. But we should always remember: protecting our space and inner peace is worth more than the fear of being alone. In fact, the people who matter will not leave. And the ones who do—maybe they were never really there for the real you in the first place.

So keep going. Even if it feels awkward. Even if people don't understand right away.

Because the truth is—**being misunderstood is not the end of the road. It's just part of the journey.**

And once you accept that, something amazing happens. You stop trying to be perfect for others. You start being real for yourself.

And that's when everything truly begins.

The Beautiful Feeling of Becoming the Owner of Your Life

If you've truly gone through those uncomfortable emotions that you had been avoiding for so long, then something starts to shift inside you. When you finally stop escaping, when you allow yourself to feel the fear of being judged or misunderstood, and when you still decide to stand for your space and your truth — that's when you touch something new.

It's not something loud or dramatic. It doesn't come with applause or big moments. But deep inside, there is a very soft, very quiet, but very beautiful feeling. It is the feeling of becoming the owner of your life.

You suddenly begin to feel lighter. It's as if some invisible weight you had been carrying for years has quietly dropped. You don't feel the need to please everyone anymore. You're not rushing to make people feel comfortable at your own cost. You're not stuck in overthinking after every little disagreement. A calmness begins to settle in. Not because the world has changed — but because you're no longer trying to bend yourself just to fit in.

You feel steady. You feel real. You feel free. This is not just confidence. This is emotional freedom. You finally feel like this life belongs to you — not to your image, not to expectations, not to fear.

It doesn't mean everything becomes perfect. There will still be tough moments. People will still misunderstand you sometimes. You will still be questioned or doubted. But even in those moments, you will feel something new — a sense that you can survive this. That you can handle discomfort. That you don't need to collapse every time someone disapproves of you. That your truth is enough — even when it's not approved by others.

This feeling doesn't come suddenly. It builds slowly. Moment by moment. Step by step. But when it arrives, you'll know it. You'll feel something has shifted inside — not in your words, but in your presence. You'll realise that you don't have to over-explain, over-smile, or over-adjust anymore. You can just be. Fully. Simply. Calmly.

You may still feel nervous while speaking your mind. Your heart may still beat faster in certain situations. But now, that fear doesn't stop you. You move with it. You carry it. But you don't let it define you anymore. And that is growth. That is ownership.

If this book has helped you see even a small part of yourself more clearly — if it helped you pause, reflect, or stand for your space even once — then that is your first success. That is your first real shift. It may look small from outside, but inside, you know how much courage it took. And that courage will stay with you.

This book was never about giving you tricks. It was not about teaching you how to be loud or aggressive. It was about helping you become emotionally honest. To bring you back to your centre. To your voice. To your space. And if you're feeling even a small connection with that space now — then you've already started owning your life.

This is your beautiful reward. Not perfection. Not performance. But peace — the kind that comes when you stop hiding and start showing up, just as you are.

Finally, A New Leader is Born

You've moved through the stages of awareness, recognition, and becoming – and now stand at the threshold of a new self.

Congratulations.

A true leader is not someone who never feels fear. A true leader is someone who moves forward even while carrying fear. And when you do that – step by step, moment by moment – you inspire others without even trying.

So now, your journey doesn't end here. In fact, it begins. You've broken free from the goody-goody trap, and you've learned to protect your emotional space. But more than that, you've unlocked the ability to lead – not just projects, teams, or families – but first, and most importantly, yourself.

Before we part, I want to thank you for walking through these pages with me. This book was never meant as advice from one person to another, but as a shared journey. My hope is that whenever you feel the old patterns tugging at you, you'll remember that you are no longer trapped. You are free, and you are leading your own life now. Wishing you strength, calm, and clarity on every step ahead.